A LITTLE

TUSCAN

COOKBOOK

To dear Thelma
with love,
Josephine
1998

MARY MAW AND RADHA PATTERSON

Illustrated by NEISHA ALLEN

CHRONICLE BOOKS

SAN FRANCISCO

First published in 1994 by
The Appletree Press Ltd
19–21 Alfred Street, Belfast BT2 8DL
Tel. +44 232 243074 Fax +44 232 246756
Copyright © 1994 The Appletree Press, Ltd.
Illustrations © 1994 The Appletree Press, Ltd.
Printed in the E.U. All rights reserved.

A Little Tuscan Cookbook

First published in the United States in 1994 by
Chronicle Books, 275 Fifth Street,
San Francisco, California 94103

ISBN 0-8118-0803-3

9 8 7 6 5 4 3 2 1

Introduction

Probably the best known of all Italian regions, Tuscany is famed for the glorious Renaissance art and architecture of its towns and cities and the beauty of its villages and countryside. Tuscan wines and olive oil are among the finest produced in Italy and Tuscan food is no less excellent. Noted for its simplicity and purity, the region's cooking stems from ancient rural traditions yet has enormous appeal for today's health-conscious cook. Meats in a Tuscan kitchen are grilled or roasted; vegetables are plainly cooked or eaten raw. Bread is consumed in great quantities, puddings are reserved for special occasions, and butter and cream are not used much. Olive oil is the major distinctive ingredient in Tuscan cooking. Rosemary and garlic provide two other typical flavors. Rice and pasta play only minor roles in the traditional Tuscan diet and meals are usually begun with a soup. Pulses in the form of cannellini beans and chick-peas are popular hence the Tuscans' nickname *I Mangiafagioli* – the bean eaters! Not much cheese is made in the region but, of Italy's ewe's milk cheeses, *Pecorino Toscano* is considered one of the finest.

The recipes chosen to represent Tuscan cooking do not require obscure ingredients or special equipment. They do call for, above all else, the best quality (preferably Tuscan) olive oil and the freshest produce available. Equipped with these, we hope our selection will allow you to recreate the flavors of Tuscany in your own kitchen and inspire you to delve further into the delights of Tuscan cooking.

Note
Recipes are for four unless otherwise indicated.

Pinzimonio

A bowl of virgin olive oil into which crunchy vegetables are dipped and then eaten is the inspiration for this simple dish. In this version, finely chopped fennel, rosemary, garlic and chili, flavors redolent of Tuscan cooking, are added to the olive oil. Served with good bread, *Pinzimonio* is a delightful introduction to Tuscan food.

1/2 large bulb of fennel
1/2 clove of garlic
1 small dried chili
sprig of fresh rosemary
1/2 cup extra-virgin olive oil
salt and freshly ground black pepper

Chop the fennel, garlic, chili and rosemary very finely (the Italian implement called *mezzaluna* is most effective for chopping). Add the olive oil, mix well, and season with salt and pepper to taste. Leave for several hours to allow flavors to mingle. Serve with slices of crusty bread or Tuscan *schiacciata* (see p. 11).

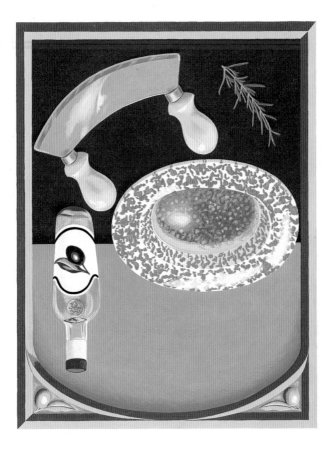

Bruschetta al Pomodoro

Ripe tomatoes, extra-virgin olive oil, and bread are the ingredients for these canapés served in *trattorie* all over Tuscany. Alas, tomatoes available elsewhere are not always as flavorsome as those grown in central Italy. A few drops of balsamic vinegar, though not strictly Tuscan, can however enliven dull tomatoes and when fresh basil is not available dried oregano is an acceptable substitute.

---

1 lb tomatoes
6 tbsp extra-virgin olive oil
a few leaves of basil torn into small pieces,
or a large pinch of dried oregano
a few drops of balsamic vinegar
salt and freshly ground black pepper
12 slices of crusty French or Italian-style bread
1 clove of garlic, peeled
(makes 12)

Using a swivel-action potato peeler remove the skin from the tomatoes with a sawing motion. Quarter tomatoes, remove the core and seeds, and chop into small pieces. Toss with half the olive oil, the basil or oregano, a few drops of balsamic vinegar, salt, and pepper. Brush the bread with the remaining olive oil, rub with the garlic clove, and toast under a hot broiler until golden brown. Top with the tomato mixture and serve at once.

Crostini di Fegatini

These delicious Tuscan *crostini* make ideal pre-dinner canapés. The chicken mixture should be eaten slightly warm and used within 24 hours.

2 tbsp olive oil	1 tbsp capers, finely chopped
1 oz butter	salt and freshly ground
1 small onion, finely chopped	black pepper
1 stick of celery, finely chopped	½ large French baguette or
½ carrot, finely chopped	Italian-style country loaf cut
8 oz chicken livers, cleaned	into 16 slices approximately
and chopped into small pieces	¾ inch thick
3 tbsp dry white wine	4 tbsp olive oil
2 anchovy fillets, finely chopped	16 gherkins

(makes 16)

Place the olive oil and half the butter in a saucepan. Melt the butter and add the finely chopped onion, celery, and carrot. Cook for 10–15 minutes, stirring frequently. When the vegetables are soft, lower the heat and add the chicken liver. Cook for a few minutes until the liver turns brown. Raise the heat, add the white wine, and simmer until it evaporates. Salt to taste, cover the pan and cook at low heat for 10–15 minutes. Remove from heat, add the anchovies, capers, pepper, and the remaining butter. Blend this mixture briefly in a food processor or chop it by hand. It should retain a granular consistency.

To make the *crostini*, brush the slices of bread with the olive oil and toast under a hot grill until golden brown. Top each slice with the chicken liver mixture and garnish with a gherkin. Serve at once.

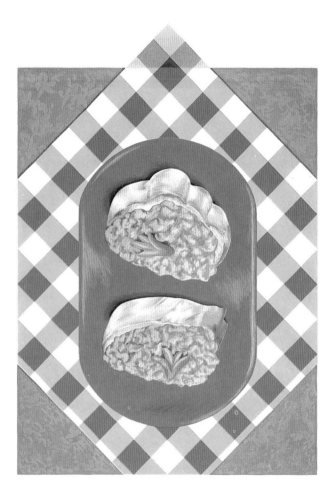

Schiacciata

Bread is a vital part of Tuscan cuisine. It is eaten not only as an accompaniment to meals but as an ingredient in soups and salads. *Schiacciata* (which means flat bread) is Tuscany's version of *focaccia*. Easy to make and very flavorsome, it can be filled to make delicious sandwiches, covered with a topping like a pizza, or simply enjoyed with antipasto or soup.

6⅓ cups strong white flour	3 tbsp olive oil
2 tsp salt	olive oil
½ oz active dried yeast	sea salt
½ oz sugar	fresh or dried rosemary
2 cups hand-hot water	

Preheat the oven to 425°F. Sift the flour and salt into a bowl. In a separate bowl, mix the yeast and sugar with ½ cup of the water. Make a well in the center of the flour. When the yeast has dissolved and begins to fizz, add the rest of the water and the olive oil and pour this mixture gradually into the flour. Mix the dough until it is soft and sticky and then turn it onto a floured surface. Cover and allow it to rest for 5 minutes. The dough should then be kneaded for 10 minutes until smooth and springy to the touch. Place the dough in a bowl, cover with plastic wrap and leave to rise in a warm place for about 2 hours until it has doubled in size. Oil a baking sheet and, when the dough has risen, knead it lightly again and form into two 12-inch circles. Put the circles on the baking sheet and leave to rise again for about 20 minutes. When the bread has risen another ½ inch or so, press fingers into the surface to create little dimples. Brush the top of the bread liberally with olive oil and sprinkle with sea salt and rosemary. Bake for 15 minutes and then reduce heat to 400°F and bake for a further 5–10 minutes. When the bread is golden brown, remove it from the oven and place on a wire rack. Using your fingers, gently spread more olive oil over the surface of the bread and allow to cool before serving.

Polpette

Polpette (meatballs) are found all over Italy but are thought to have originated in Tuscany. They can be made with almost any type of cooked meat, though minced veal and pork are the most commonly used. *Prosciutto* is often combined with the meat, though in this recipe mortadella sausage is used, with delicious results. Served with a salad, *polpette* make a splendid light lunch. They are also excellent as pre-dinner canapés.

6 oz cooked breast of chicken	salt and pepper
3 oz mortadella sausage	1 egg, beaten
1 clove garlic, finely chopped	breadcrumbs
2 oz grated Parmesan cheese	sunflower or arachide oil for frying
1 tbsp parsley, finely chopped	lemon wedges
4 oz boiled potato, mashed	
(makes 12–16)	

Blend the cooked breast of chicken and mortadella sausage in a food processor for a couple of minutes. Empty into a bowl and mix in the chopped garlic, Parmesan cheese, parsley, and the mashed potato. Season with salt and pepper and bind the paste with the beaten egg. Shape the mixture into small balls or sausage shapes, roll in breadcrumbs, and fry in the hot oil until crisp and golden. Drain on paper towels and serve immediately with wedges of lemon.

Panzanella

This rustic salad was orginally made with bread soaked in water, but is now made from cubes of bread toasted in olive oil to make a classic Tuscan dish that can be a sophisticated first course or a light lunch.

Croutons

4 oz crusty French or Italian-style bread	2 tbsp extra-virgin olive oil salt

---

Preheat the oven to 400°F. Cube the bread into 1-inch pieces. Place the cubes of bread on a large baking sheet and drizzle the olive oil over them, ensuring they are well covered. Sprinkle lightly with salt. Bake the croutons until crisp and brown (10–15 minutes). Check them every few minutes as they burn easily.

Panzanella

1/2 clove garlic	1/2 red onion, finely sliced
1 tbsp capers	1 yellow pepper, seeds and pulpy
2 flat anchovy fillets	core removed, and cut into
5 tbsp extra-virgin olive oil	2 inch cubes
salt and freshly ground black pepper	1/2 cucumber, halved length-ways and cut into slices
1 tbsp red wine vinegar	10 basil leaves, torn into small
1 quantity of croutons	pieces
3 firm, ripe tomatoes, seeded and cut into 1 inch strips	

To make the dressing, combine the garlic, capers, anchovies, oil, salt, and vinegar in a food processor and blend to a smooth consistency. Place the croutons, vegetables, and basil leaves in a

bowl and pour over the dressing. Add several grindings of black pepper, toss thoroughly, and serve at once.

Tonno e Fagioli

This popular dish combines Tuscany's beloved beans with canned tuna fish to produce a substantial salad suitable for a first course or light lunch. Canned cannellini beans may be used but the texture and flavor of cooked dried beans is vastly superior.

14 oz dried cannellini beans	juice of 1/2 a lemon
1 onion, peeled	3 6 oz cans of tuna in olive oil
1 bay leaf	1/2 red onion, cut into thin slices
salt and freshly ground	small bunch of parsley,
black pepper	finely chopped
2/3 cup olive oil	

Soak the cannellini beans in cold water for 5–6 hours or overnight. Discard the soaking water and place beans in large saucepan together with onion and bay leaf. Cover with water and bring to a boil. Remove any scum that floats to the surface. Reduce to a simmer, cover and cook for 40–60 minutes. The cooking time depends on the age of the beans – the older the beans, the longer the cooking time – so test them every now and again. Add salt to taste at the end of the cooking time.

When the beans are tender, but not mushy, drain them and discard the onion and the bay leaf. While still warm, put the beans into a large bowl and dress with the olive oil, salt, pepper, and the lemon juice. Add the drained tuna, using a fork to break it into

chunks, and the finely sliced onion. Toss the ingredients to mix well, garnish with chopped parsley and serve.

Passata di Peperone

This recipe for roasted yellow pepper soup is based on a traditional Tuscan country recipe. It is ideal with thick, crusty bread which has been brushed with extra-virgin olive oil and then grilled.

---

2 lb 2 oz yellow peppers
2 tbsp olive oil
1 medium onion, finely chopped
1 carrot, finely chopped
1 stick celery, finely chopped
2 medium potatoes, peeled and diced
4 1/2 cups chicken stock
salt and freshly ground black pepper

Roast the peppers by putting them under a hot broiler until the skin is blistered all over. Let them cool, then peel off the charred skin. De-seed, cut into strips, and set aside.

Put the olive oil into a deep saucepan and add the chopped onion, carrot, and celery. Sauté until the vegetables-soften. Add the yellow peppers and sauté for a further 10 minutes, then add the potatoes and chicken stock. Bring to a boil, lower heat, and simmer for 30 minutes. Purée the vegetables and add salt and pepper to taste. Drizzle some olive oil on to the soup and serve at once.

Minestra di Pasta e Ceci

This soup is found all over central Italy. There are many recipes for it, but this is a typically Tuscan version. It is a very rich soup, and should be served in small quantities.

---

1 cup chick-peas
3 tbsp extra-virgin olive oil
1 medium onion, peeled and chopped
1 medium carrot, diced
1 stick celery, chopped
3 cloves of garlic, crushed
8 cups water
¹/₂ cup pasta such as stelline or tiny macaroni
salt and freshly ground black pepper
chili-flavored olive oil (optional)

Place the chick-peas in a bowl and pour boiling water over them. Leave to soak for one hour. Put oil in large saucepan and add chopped vegetables and garlic. Cook for about 10 minutes over a moderate heat until soft. Add the drained chick-peas and stir to coat with oil. Pour in the water, cover, and bring to a simmer. Simmer until chick-peas are tender (1–2 hours). Be sure to stir the soup from time to time to prevent the vegetables from sticking. When the chick-peas are tender, purée them. The soup should be creamy in texture but not entirely smooth. Add the pasta, salt and black pepper and cook for a further 10 minutes, stirring frequently. A few drops of olive oil flavored with chili greatly enlivens this soup.

Pappa al Pomodoro

A traditional Tuscan dish, this dense, flavorsome soup is found all over the region. Made with plenty of garlic, ripe tomatoes, extra-virgin olive oil, and fresh basil, it is the perfect first course on a summer evening.

---

1 cup extra-virgin olive oil
2 medium onions, finely sliced
2 tsp sugar
8 cloves of garlic, finely chopped
1 crushed dried red chili pepper
1 lb tomatoes, peeled and chopped
4 tbsp tomato paste
10 leaves of basil – more if you prefer
4 1/2 cups vegetable stock
salt and pepper to taste
1 lb country-style bread (1–2 days old) torn into small pieces

---

Heat the oil in a deep saucepan and fry the onion until it is soft, but not brown. Add the sugar and cook for 5 minutes. Put in the garlic and chili pepper . When these soften (about 10 minutes), add the tomatoes, the tomato paste, and the basil leaves and cook for a further 10 minutes. Put in the stock and the seasoning. After the mixture has come to a boil, add the bread. Simmer for 40 minutes over a low heat, stirring from time to time. Mix well before serving and pour on some olive oil. Serve warm or at room temperature, garnished with basil leaves.

Pinci con Sugo di Salsiccia

Fresh pasta is not traditionally part of Tuscan cooking. In the Siena area, however, *pinci*, a kind of handmade spaghetti, is found. Not a dish for those in a hurry as each strand of pasta is rolled by hand, *pinci* is nonetheless worth the effort and makes the perfect partner for a robust sauce made with meaty Italian sausage.

Pinci

3 cups strong white flour	1–1 $^1/_2$ cups cold water
pinch of salt	1 tbsp olive oil

Place the flour and salt in a mound on a flat surface and make a well in the center. Pour on some of the water and draw in the flour from the edge. Repeat this process until the dough is firm but sticky, using more water if necessary. Add the olive oil and knead the dough for 2–3 minutes until smooth and springy to the touch. Flatten the dough to a thickness of $^1/_2$ inch. Cut it into $^1/_2$-inch strips and then into $^1/_2$-inch cubes. Take each cube and using finger and thumb flatten out to about 3-inch length. Then, using the palms of the hand, roll each length of the pasta dough into rounded strips about 8–9 inches long. Place on cotton towels until ready to use. To cook, bring a large saucepan of water to a boil. Add the *pinci* and boil for 1–3 minutes until *al dente*.

Sauce

1 tbsp extra-virgin olive oil	salt and freshly ground
2 cloves of garlic, finely chopped	black pepper
8 oz meaty sausages	2 oz freshly grated
(preferably Italian), skinned	Parmesan cheese
14 oz can Italian tomatoes,	
chopped	

PINCI

Put the oil and garlic into a skillet and sauté until the garlic is golden. Add the sausages, using a fork to break them up. Cook until the sausages are well browned. Add the tomatoes and simmer until they separate from the oil. Season with salt and pepper and use the sauce to dress the *pinci*. Serve with the grated Parmesan cheese.

Penne all'Arrabiata

The dried pasta shape most characteristic of the Tuscan region is *penne*, so-called because of its quill-like shape. The sauce is described as *arrabiata,* which means angry because it is "enraged" with chili, a spice commonly used in the area but confusingly called *zenzero* which is the name for ginger elsewhere in Italy.

2 tbsp extra-virgin olive oil	1 lb penne
2 cloves of garlic, finely chopped	a few leaves of basil torn into
1 dried chili pepper, crushed	small pieces
2 oz pancetta, cut into	1 oz Parmesan cheese, grated
narrow strips	1 oz pecorino cheese, grated
2 14 oz cans of tomatoes,	
chopped	

Put the olive oil in a large skillet and add the garlic and chili. When the garlic begins to color, add the *pancetta* and fry until it is brown but not crisp. Add the chopped tomatoes and simmer for about half an hour until they separate from the oil. Cook the *penne* in a large saucepan of salted boiling water until *al dente*. Add the basil to the sauce and cook for a few more minutes. Drain the pasta, add the sauce and the cheeses, and serve at once.

Manzo Brasato al Chianti

This delicious recipe for beef cooked in wine is found all over Italy and dates as far back as the sixteenth century. Chianti Classico, the great wine of the region south of Florence, is used here to give the meat its excellent flavor.

---

2 lb 2 oz topside of beef, all in one piece
4 fat cloves of garlic cut in slivers
2 oz pancetta
3 tbsp olive oil
1 carrot, diced
1 stick celery, diced
1 medium onion, thinly sliced
2 wine glasses Chianti or other red wine
salt and freshly ground black pepper

With a sharp knife make several slits in the beef and insert a sliver of garlic and a sliver of *pancetta* into each slit. Put the olive oil into a large casserole dish and brown the beef in it. Add the chopped vegetables and let them soften. Pour in the wine and the seasoning and bring to a boil. Lower the heat and cover. The beef should simmer for 3–4 hours and the heat should be so low that barely a bubble breaks the surface. At the end of the cooking time, remove the meat, cut it into thick slices, spoon the sauce over it, and serve at once.

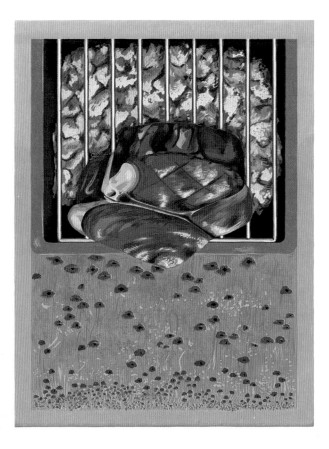

Bistecca alla Fiorentina

One of the best known dishes of Tuscany is the Florentine *bistecca* – a thick T-bone steak which is lightly grilled over charcoal and eaten *al sangue* (very rare). The success of this dish depends on the quality of the meat and Tuscan beef is considered to be particularly fine. It can be cooked either on a barbecue or in a broiler.

---

2 very large T-bone steaks – 1 1/2 lb each
1 tbsp olive oil
salt and freshly ground black pepper

Heat the broiler and, when very hot, lay the steaks side by side under it. Broil for 4 minutes or until the meat darkens. Turn the steaks over and season with salt and black pepper and cook the second side for a further 4 minutes. If you do not like the meat rare, cook for a further 2 minutes. Brush the steaks with olive oil and serve immediately.

Agnello col Olive Nere

This dish originates from Lucca – an area famous for its olives – and variations are found all over Tuscany. This recipe includes dried red chili pepper – a flavor typical of Tuscan cooking.

---

3 tbsp oil
2 cloves garlic, finely chopped
2 sprigs fresh rosemary
2 lb 2 oz shoulder of lamb, cubed
2 wine glasses of dry white wine
6 large ripe tomatoes, peeled and chopped
1 tbsp of grated lemon rind
1 dried red chili pepper
4 oz of pitted black olives
salt and freshly ground black pepper

Heat the oil in a wide pan, add the garlic and rosemary, and cook until the garlic colors. Put in the cubes of lamb and turn them in the hot oil until they brown. Pour in the wine and when it has reduced to half, add the tomatoes, the lemon rind, and the chili pepper. Cover and simmer over a low heat for about 20 minutes. Add the olives, cover again, and cook for a further hour or so, stirring from time to time to prevent the meat from sticking. Add a little water if the stew gets too dry. At the end of the cooking time, the meat should be moist and tender.

Arista alla Fiorentina

According to legend, the Greek bishops who served this dish at an ecumenical council held in Florence in 1430 pronounced it *aristos*, the Greek word for "best". This roast loin of pork is indeed exceedingly good.

---

3 tbsp olive oil
4 cloves of garlic, peeled
6 sage leaves
leaves from 2 sprigs of rosemary
salt and freshly ground black pepper
3 lb boneless loin of pork with a good covering of fat

Preheat the oven to 400°F. Combine the oil, garlic, herbs and seasoning in a food processor and blend together. Rub the oil and herb mixture over the pork, making incisions in the fat and pushing the mixture into them. Roll the pork up tightly and tie at intervals with string. Roast for 1½–2 hours on a wire rack until the juices run clear. Carve into slices and serve at once.

Pollo al Diavolo

The best free-range Italian chickens are said to come from Tuscany and Tuscan cooks are regarded as experts at preparing delicious chicken dishes. Like so much Tuscan food, this dish is simplicity itself but calls for a top quality free-range bird. It is best barbecued, but can be cooked very successfully in a broiler.

---

olive oil
juice of 1 lemon
1/2 dried red chili pepper (crushed)
salt and freshly ground black pepper
3–3 1/2 lb chicken

Mix together olive oil, lemon juice, crushed chili, salt, and pepper. Split the chicken open along the breast and flatten as much as possible. Cover with the marinade and leave for at least one hour. Barbecue or broil for 30–40 minutes, brushing occasionally with the marinade until the juices from the thigh run clear.

Petti di Pollo con Salsa di Dragoncello

Tarragon is not a herb usually associated with Italian cooking, but in the area around Siena it appears in some dishes – hence its other name, *erba di Siena*. The sauce in this recipe usually accompanies boiled meats but is delicious served with chicken.

1 tbsp flour
salt and freshly ground black pepper
4 chicken breasts, boned and skinned
2 oz butter

Mix flour, salt, and pepper together and dust over chicken breasts. Heat the butter in a large skillet and when it has melted, add the chicken breasts and fry on both sides until brown. Reduce heat, cover the pan, and cook the breasts for a further 15–20 minutes.

Sauce
1 1/2 oz fresh white breadcrumbs
1 clove of garlic, finely chopped
2 tbsp parsley, finely chopped
large bunch of tarragon, finely chopped
1 hard-boiled egg yolk, well mashed
salt and freshly ground black pepper
1/2 cup extra-virgin olive oil
1 tbsp red wine vinegar

Soak the breadcrumbs in water for 5 minutes. Combine the garlic, parsley, and tarragon in a bowl. Squeeze the water out of the breadcrumbs and add to the chopped herbs along with the egg yolk, salt, and pepper. Slowly drizzle the olive oil onto this mixture, stirring constantly, until the sauce is smooth and even. Refrigerate for an hour or so, add the vinegar, and serve the chicken accompanied by the sauce.

Sogliole alla Fiorentina

Spinach features prominently in Tuscan cuisine, and the word "Florentine" is now a standard culinary term describing eggs or fish served on a bed of spinach. This classic recipe calls for sole, but plaice or other white fish are just as suitable.

---

2 lb 2 oz fresh spinach, or 1 lb frozen spinach, thawed
5 oz butter
salt and freshly ground black pepper
pinch of grated nutmeg
1 glass dry white wine
8 fillets of sole
2 oz all-purpose flour
2 cups hot milk
3 oz grated Parmesan cheese

Preheat the oven to 400°F. If you are using fresh spinach, wash the leaves thoroughly and place in a saucepan with 1 oz of the butter. Cook briefly until the leaves wilt. Season with salt, pepper and grated nutmeg. If you are using frozen spinach, thaw in a saucepan over moderate heat, drain and squeeze out all the moisture. Add 1 oz butter and season as above.

Melt 2 oz butter in a skillet and add the wine. Warm through for a few minutes and then add the sole. Cook the sole fillets for about 7 minutes, remove from skillet and boil the wine briskly until it has reduced by half. In a small saucepan, melt the remaining butter, add the flour and mix thoroughly to form a smooth *roux*. Gradually add the hot milk, stirring as you do and let the mixture

thicken. Season with salt and pepper and more nutmeg. Put in the reduced wine mixture and stir until well mixed. Grease an ovenproof gratin dish and cover the base with the spinach. Lay the fish on top and coat with the sauce. Sprinkle with the Parmesan cheese and bake for 15–20 minutes until a golden crust has formed over the top.

Trote alla Griglia

The many rivers which flow through the Tuscan countryside ensure a rich supply of freshwater fish in inland areas. Trout is the most popular, and in this recipe it is served grilled in the Tuscan fashion.

---

4 oz white breadcrumbs
2 cloves of garlic, finely chopped
few leaves of rosemary, finely chopped
bunch of parsley, finely chopped
salt and freshly ground black pepper
extra-virgin olive oil
4 brown or rainbow trout, cleaned, but with heads left on

Briefly soak the breadcrumbs in water and then squeeze them dry. Combine the breadcrumbs, garlic, rosemary, parsley, salt, pepper, and a little olive oil in a food processor and mix to a paste-like consistency. Wash and dry the cavities of the trout and stuff with this mixture. Close with toothpicks. Brush the fish with olive oil and sprinkle with salt. Grill on a barbecue or under a hot broiler, basting the trout with the olive oil from time to time.

Patate al Forno

Although not an everyday food, potatoes are featured in northern Italian cooking. This recipe combines the basic Tuscan ingredients of olive oil, rosemary and garlic with potatoes to produce a dish which is the perfect partner for the region's broiled and roasted meats.

---

1 1/2 lb small, new potatoes
6 tbsp olive oil
2 sprigs of rosemary
2 cloves of garlic, peeled
salt and freshly ground black pepper

Preheat the oven to 400°F. Wash the potatoes and boil until just tender and then drain. Put the oil, rosemary, and garlic into a baking dish and warm in oven for 5 minutes. Add the potatoes, a generous sprinkling of salt and some pepper. Bake for 20–30 minutes, turning from time to time until the skins are golden brown.

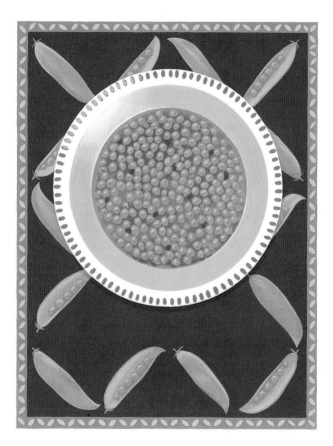

Piselli alla Toscana

Garden peas are thought to have been developed in Italy in the sixteenth century and it is said that they were one of Catherine de Medici's favorite foods. Unless you grow your own, fresh garden peas are not easily found. This Tuscan recipe, however, turns even the humble frozen pea into something special.

---

2 cloves garlic, peeled
2 tbsp extra-virgin olive oil
2 tbsp pancetta or prosciutto, finely chopped
2 lb 2 oz garden peas, shelled or
10 oz frozen peas, defrosted
2 tbsp parsley, finely chopped
salt and freshly ground black pepper

Sauté the garlic in the olive oil until golden brown and then remove from the saucepan with a slotted spoon. Add the *pancetta* and cook for a few minutes. Pour in the peas and turn them in the oil. Put in the parsley, salt, and pepper to taste. If using fresh peas, add a little water. Reduce the heat and cook the peas until tender, 15–30 minutes if fresh, 5 minutes if frozen.

Fagioli a l'Ucelletto

Tuscans are sometimes described as *I Mangiafagioli,* or bean eaters, because of their fondness for beans. Cannellini is the variety most frequently used in this typically Tuscan recipe which makes an ideal companion to the roast loin of pork. The beans must be soaked overnight.

---

2 cups cannellini beans soaked
for 5-6 hours or overnight
1 onion, peeled
6 tbsp olive oil
2 sprigs of sage
2 cloves of garlic, peeled
14 oz can of tomatoes
salt and freshly ground black pepper

Drain the beans and put them in a large saucepan. Cover with cold water and bring to a boil. Cook for 3 minutes. Drain and rinse the beans and return to the pan with the onion. Cover with cold water and return to a boil. Let the beans simmer until tender – about 40 minutes to 1 hour. Five minutes or so before the end of cooking, add salt to taste, drain the beans, and discard the onion. In a medium saucepan, heat the oil together with the sage leaves and garlic. Add the tomatoes and simmer for 10 minutes and then add the beans. Season with salt and pepper and simmer for another 15–20 minutes.

Zucchini al Forno

Zucchini is popular throughout Italy and zucchini fields in bloom are a glorious sight in the Tuscan countryside.

This dish makes a wonderful light summer lunch and goes very well with *insalata verde* (see p. 52) and crusty bread. It is good served hot or cold.

---

4 large or 8 small zucchini
2–3 tbsp all-purpose flour
³/₄ cup vegetable oil
8 eggs beaten
4 tbsp milk
salt and freshy ground black pepper
4 oz freshly grated Parmesan cheese
2 tbsp fresh basil leaves, roughly torn
3 tbsp fresh white breadcrumbs

Preheat the oven to 375°F. Top and tail the zucchini and then cut lengthwise into ¹/₂-inch slices. Coat the slices lightly in the flour and fry in hot oil until they are crisp and golden. Drain on paper towels. Oil a round ovenproof dish and arrange the zucchini slices like the spokes of a wheel. Beat together the eggs, milk, salt, pepper, and half the cheese. Add the basil leaves and pour this mixture over the zucchini. Sprinkle the breadcrumbs and the remaining Parmesan cheese over the top. Bake the zucchini in the oven for about 15–20 minutes until the top is just firm to the touch.

Insalata Verde

A green salad served after the second course is an essential part of a Tuscan meal. The components of the salad will change according to seasonal availability of lettuces, radicchio, rocket, or other green leaves, but the dressing never varies.

A perfectly dressed salad requires salt, extra-virgin Tuscan olive oil, and good quality wine vinegar. Marcella Hazan, in *The Essentials of Classic Italian Cooking*, quotes a proverb which says four persons are required for a good salad: a judicious one for the salt, a prodigal one for the olive oil, a stingy one for the vinegar, and a patient one to toss. These ingredients are never mixed in advance but added at the table in the order given and the salad is served at once.

Ricotta al Caffe

Ricotta, a soft cheese made from whey, is produced throughout Italy. It is used in puddings, as a filling for pasta and savory tarts or eaten on its own. This Tuscan recipe, originally a *merenda,* or mid-morning dish, makes a delicious dessert.

---

12 oz ricotta
5 oz confectioner's sugar
3 tbsp strong black coffee
2 tbsp brandy, or other spirits, to taste
grated chocolate or cocoa powder

Combine the *ricotta*, confectioner's sugar, coffee, and brandy in a food processor and blend very briefly. Leave for an hour or so to

allow the flavors to develop. To serve, line four ramekin dishes with plastic wrap and fill with the *ricotta* cream. Turn over onto dessert plates and unmold. Sprinkle each pudding with grated chocolate or cocoa powder and serve at once.

Torta a Riso

Rice is not featured largely in traditional Tuscan cooking, but arborio rice is used to make cakes and puddings. This rice cake is best made one day in advance and keeps well if it is wrapped in aluminum foil and stored in a cool place. *Amaretti* are crispy, almond-flavored cookies. In this recipe they make a welcome alternative to plain breadcrumbs.

---

1 1/2 cups milk
strip of lemon peel
6 oz superfine sugar
few drops of vanilla extract or a piece of vanilla bean
a pinch of salt
5 oz arborio rice
4 eggs separated
2 oz candied peel, finely chopped
2 tbsp brandy
butter for greasing cake pan
2 pairs amaretti *cookies, crushed*
confectioner's sugar for dusting

Preheat oven to 350°F. Place milk, lemon peel, superfine sugar, vanilla, and salt in a medium-size saucepan. Bring to a boil and add the rice. Cook over low heat until the rice has absorbed all the milk, stirring from time to time. Allow to cool, remove lemon peel and, if using, the vanilla bean. Mix in egg yolks, candied peel, and brandy. Whisk egg whites until stiff and fold into the rice mixture. Grease an 8-inch spring-form pan with butter and sprinkle the bottom and sides with *amaretti* crumbs. Spoon in rice mixture and bake for 45 minutes to 1 hour until cake is golden. Allow cake to cool in the pan. When cold, unmold and store in a cool place for 24 hours. Before serving, dust with confectioner's sugar. A fruit purée, such as raspberry or apricot, goes very well with this cake.

Zuccotto

A specialty of Florence, this dome-shaped pudding may have been inspired by the great cupola of the Duomo which dominates the skyline of the city. Stunning to look at and wickedly rich, it is a spectacular dessert. It should be made one day in advance.

---

1 9 oz rectangular madeira or sponge cake
3 tbsp cointreau, 3 tbsp brandy (mixed together)
6 oz dark chocolate
3$^1/_3$ cups heavy cream
2 oz confectioner's sugar
3 oz glacé fruits, chopped into small pieces

Line a 4-cup bowl with plastic wrap. Cut the cake lengthwise into slices about $^1/_4$-inch thick and line the bowl with them, working as neatly as possible, filling all gaps. Sprinkle the cake with the cointreau and brandy mixture. Chop 4 oz of the chocolate into

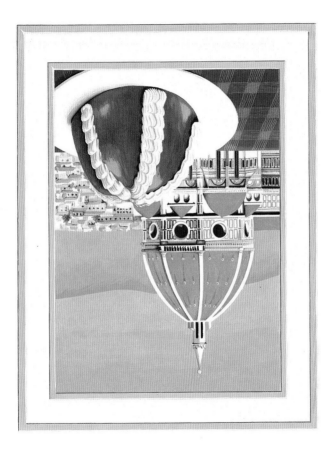

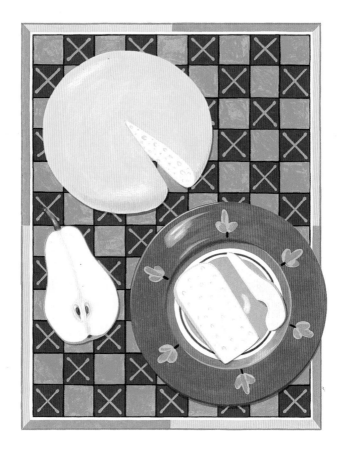

small pieces. Whip half the cream and the confectioner's sugar together until stiff and add the glacé fruits and half the chopped chocolate. Spread half this mixture over the cake leaving a well in the center. Melt the rest of the chopped chocolate in a bowl over simmering water, fold it into the remaining cream and fruit mixture and fill the hollow in the center of the pudding. Use the rest of the cake to make a lid for the pudding. Cover with plastic wrap and refrigerate overnight. Before serving, unmold the pudding onto a plate. Whip the remaining cream until stiff. Melt the remaining 2 oz of the chocolate and mix with $^3/_4$ of the cream. Spread the chocolate cream over the pudding, smoothing with a palette knife as you go along. Put the remaining cream into a piping bag and pipe five lines of cream from the top of the pudding to the base at equal intervals. Keep refrigerated until served.

Pere e Pecorino

Pecorino is an ewe's milk cheese produced all over central and southern Italy. Those made in Tuscany are held by many to be the most superior of the pecorinos. The cheese made in the area south of Siena known as *pecorino della crete senesi* is highly regarded. Pecorino from the Pienza area is also considered excellent. Tuscan pecorino can be eaten when it is two weeks old or when aged for six months. Traditionally, it is enjoyed at the end of a meal with fresh broad beans when they are in season. It is also delicious served with juicy ripe pears whose flavor complements very well the piquancy of the pecorino.

Index